"Some educators believe that up to 80% of what a child learns during the school year can be lost after 48 hours . . ."

Dear Parent,

Picking up this book shows that you are interested in your child's reading abilities, and that you have accepted the challenge of working with your child during a time when education may take a back seat to other adventures.

Summer is the perfect time to reinforce reading skills taught during the school year. Some educators believe that up to 80% of what a child learns can be lost after 48 hours if not reinforced aggressively and consistently. Think of what 12 weeks away from school will do!

Summer Bridge Reading Activities is designed to help children have fun while maintaining and extending reading skills while away from school. Each workbook consists of a variety of stories and poems which review reading skills from the grade the child is leaving, and previews skills which will be introduced in the upcoming year. *Summer Bridge Reading Activities* builds reading confidence, making the transition to the new school year easier. Phonemic awareness and controlled vocabularies are used to reinforce word recognition, contractions, compound words, recognizing details, and sequencing.

This summer, take an active interest in your child's education. Even though school books and homework are set aside, and curfews may be extended, it is important to remember that you as a parent are the most important teacher your child will ever have, and that it is necessary to challenge your child's mind even when school bells are silent.

Happy Summer Learning!

George Starks
Creative Director

Table of Contents

Remember that it is always a good idea to read the stories more than once. This builds good reading skills, fluency and comprehension. You may want to spend more than 1 or 2 days on the stories and follow-up activities!

Parent Tips

Beginning and young readers have a lot to learn about what reading is and how it works. Letters, sounds, associations, and word recognition are all new concepts and may be a bit overwhelming at times. With reassurance, patience, and willingness to help your child overcome their insecurities, their learning experience and love of reading will be drastically heightened. Summer is the perfect time to develop your parent-child reading relationship!

1. Fill a paper bag or shoe box with letters of the alphabet or simple words. Have your child draw them out one at a time. They keep the ones the know, and put the ones back that they don't know. After drawing all the letters or words, review the ones they do not know before putting them back into the bag or box. Add variety to this activity by using a timer to see how many they can solve in a certain amount of time.

2. Write letters on index cards and place them on a table. Choose one such as C and say "CAT." Have your child choose another letter such as R, and have them make up their own word using the ending you used. Example- you say "CAT" they say "RAT." Use a variety of words, and even make up your own.

3. Use alphabet cards to make simple words for your child. Leave off a letter, say the word, and have your child find the missing letter and place it where it needs to go to complete the word you originally chose.

4. Find some wooden cubes and write letters on each side with a marker. Place the cubes in a plastic cup, shake it, and toss them on a table, floor, or any flat surface. Ask your child to make words out of the letters which are showing.

5. Give your child index cards and have them write the words they are studying on one card at a time, then have them draw a picture to go with the letter they wrote. Play the memory game where you turn all the cards over and take turns trying to match the word with the picture.

6. Write words on a index cards and place them in a paper bag. Have your child draw them out one at a time, say the words. When they have several out of the bag see if they can make a sentence with the words. They do not need to use all the words, just the words needed to make a complete sentence.

7. Have your child do daily reading related activities working with words they have not yet mastered. Keep the words they know in a separate "BRAG," or "I CAN DO STACK." Add words to this stack as they master them. This helps them take pride in how well they are doing.

8. Read a story "to" your child, then take turns reading the story "with" your child. You read a line, then have them read the line after you. Alternate for the entire story.

Learning to read is like learning to ride a bicycle! Practice makes perfect!

Summer Reading List
3rd to 4th Grade

Billy and Blaze (and others),
Anderson

Mr. Popper's Penguins,
Atwater

The Bears' Vacation (and others),
Berrenstain

Superfudge (and others),
Blume

Katy and Big Snow,
Burton

The Golly Sisters Go West (series),
Byars

Cloudy with a Chance of Meatballs,
Catling

Romona Quimby, Age 8 (and others),
Cleary

Courage of Sarah Noble,
Dalgliesh

Legend of the Blue Bonnet,
DePaula

The Hardy Boys (series),
Dickson

First Trip to the Moon,
Moonwalk

Nattie Parson's Good Luck Lamb,
Earnst

My Father's Dragon (and others),
Gannett

Helen Keller,
Graff

Baseball's Best: Five Stories,
Gutelle,

Girl From the Snow Country,
Hidaka

Perfect the Pig,
Jeschke

No Coins, Please,
Korman

Witch Hunt,
Krensky

Grasshopper on the Road,
Label

A Wrinkle in Time,
L'Engel

The Horse and his Boy,
Lewis

Sarah, Plain and Tall,
MacLachlan

Dinosaur Hunters,
McMullan

Jackie Robinson & the Story of All-Black Baseball,
O'Conner

Moonhorse,
Osborne

Wump World (and others),
Peet

Dogzilla (and others),
Pilkey

Deputy Dan (series),
Rosenbloom

The Cricket in Times Square,
Selden

Chocolate Fever,
Smith

Animal Cafe,
Stadler

Emma's Dragon Hunt,
Stock

Lyle, Lyle, Crocodile,
Waber

Charlotte's Web,
White

The Castle in the Attic (and others),
Winthrop

Tongues of Jade (and others),
Yep

Summer Reading
Contract & Calendar

My parents and I decided that if I complete my
Summer Bridge Reading Activities book and
read _____ minutes per day, for 20 days, my reward
or incentive will be _____

Child's Signature_____ Parent's Signature_____

Jorgie's Jive

You can do it! I'll be helping
you along the way!
Summer Reading is fun
and helps you grow!

Day	Book	Minutes	Parent Initials	Day	Book	Minutes	Parent Initials
1				11			
2				12			
3				13			
4				14			
5				15			
6				16			
7				17			
8				18			
9				19			
10				20			

The Stray Hero

My Mom is always taking in stray animals. She sets saucers of food out on the grass in case some unfortunate animal gets dropped off and is hungry. Animals just seem to sense that our house is a safe refuge from life's woes. She bandages injured animals that have received the worst end of a fight. She makes sure they get their shots and that the vet checks them over thoroughly. After she's done all this and no one has claimed them, she puts them up for adoption. We have had as high as eleven stray animals around our house at one time.

We had this one pathetic looking kitten. It was probably the dirtiest, skinniest, mangiest looking animal I've ever seen. Mom took pity on the poor little thing. She took special care to see that it got plenty of warm milk and water. She even purchased special high protein kitty chow for it.

My dad said, "You're crazy, Edith. You'll spend all this money on it, give it a huge amount of attention, get attached to it and some kid will come along and claim it." Mom spat right back, "There's no way that anyone who abused or mistreated their kitten the way they did this one would ever ask for it back. Beside that," she added, "they would never recognize it, anyhow." Mom was right. No one came and laid claim to the cat we now call Hero.

One night, we were all sound asleep after an exhausting day. We were kind of cranky and certainly did not want to be disturbed. It was around two in the morning, when I heard this loud meowing. Next, came the wet tongue on my face. I slapped at the cat and told him to leave me alone. Then, he went to my dad with the same result.

Mom is a real heavy sleeper so it took the cat longer to get her attention. He got right by her ear and meowed as loud and as long as he could muster. He followed up with licking her face. Finally, she became fully awake. She sat up responding to the situation. Something must be wrong with the cat, she thought to herself. I might as well get up and take care of the situation. It was then that she smelled gas. She woke up dad. They turned the gas off, opened all the windows and tried to awaken me. Dad called 911, because they could not revive me, I was that far gone.

The ambulance and paramedics arrived! They worked on me all the way to the hospital. I regained consciousness, waking up in the hospital. It had been a close call!

Mom and dad explained all that had happened. We apparently had a gas leak and no one smelled it but our stray cat. We could have been asphyxiated or the whole place could have exploded!

This was one time that dad had to admit that he was thankful to a stray animal. He decided that this one was a keeper. If he was a keeper he needed a name. That's how our cat, Hero got his name!

Jorgie's Jive

Remember to read the stories more than once.
This builds good reading skills by helping you better understand what you are reading.

Follow up activities for "The Stray Hero"

1. Mark the best definition for the following words.

stray
___beggar
___unwanted
___wandered off
___unliked

exhausting
___wonder
___tired out
___warmed
___excused

mangy
___scruffy
___bitten
___slick
___rotten

pathetic
___poor
___ugly
___strange
___pitiful

refuge
___shelter
___scared
___escaped
___harmed

disturbed
___divided
___strained
___separate
___interrupted

2. Choose the correct verb:

He _____ received the worst of the fight. have had

The kitty _____ away from home. ran run

She made sure he _____ his shot. get got

He _____ the dirtiest animal around. was were

Dad _____ pit on my friend. took take

I have never _____ anything like it. saw seen

You need to _____ it a bath. gave give

Some child _____ along to buy it. come came

3. Circle all the words that are nouns.

ham	sandwich	running
mother	elephant	throw
catch	celery	mustard
seasons	jumping	wonder
naive	injured	animals
dropped	vet	adopt
hungry	special	water
money	attention	recognize
disturbed	awake	face
tongue	hero	friend
decide	admit	

4. What did Dad discourage Mom from helping the kitten?

5. Why did Dad not get up when the cat meowed?

6. Why did they open all the windows?

WRITING PROMPT: Write another adventure of a poor unfortunate animal that has a happy ending. Where does it take place? Who's involved in the story? Why did it happen?

7

Going to Work With Dad

David was dressing for school one morning when his dad popped his head in the door. "David," he smiled, "You're not going to school today." "I'm not?" David asked. "No, you're coming to work with me instead," his father told him. "Today is a special day when children get to go to work with their parents. Now, let's go!"

David danced a little jig and ran out after his father. He struggled with school and was happy for the chance to do something else. "Neat!" he exclaimed. "Do we get to take the train?" he asked his father. "Yes, David. We take the train all the way into the city." David and his father arrived at the train station. His dad bought two round-trip tickets and they climbed on board.

David sat on a leather seat by the window to watch the sprawling countryside turn into the city. The train chugged along, occasionally blowing it's whistle. They passed houses and apartments, stores and shopping malls. Soon they entered a tunnel. It was dark and the train shook gently. When they emerged out the other side, they were at their stop. "This is it," David's father said and they both got up and exited the train.

David and his father walked several blocks to the office building where his dad worked. Everything looked unfamiliar to David. There were tourists window shopping, taxis racing by and men selling peanuts from carts along the street. It was new! It was magical!

Soon they were at the office building. They entered the lobby and took the elevator to the fiftieth floor. They walked to an office in the corner and opened the door. The view out the windows was amazing! David could see for miles and miles. It felt like he was on top of the world.

David's father had to work but let David play on the computer, call his mother from the speaker phone and draw pictures of the buildings out the window. Since David's dad was an architect, David decided he wanted to be one, too! He figured he better practice his drawings so he could be an excellent architect one day!

Soon it was five o'clock and time to leave. David and his father went back down the elevator and walked to the train station. They got on board and the train pulled away from the station.

"See, if you work hard at school, you can someday be an architect who works in the city, too," David's father told him. "If you work hard and not give up, you can be almost any thing you want to be." David thought about that and decided right there and then to try harder in school, to not give up on himself. He fell asleep in seat and dreamed about working in a big office that overlooked the city, way high up in the sky!

Jorgie's Jive

Do you know what type of work your Dad does? Ask him about it? Have you ever thought about doing this type of work when you are older?

Follow-up Activities for "Going to Work With Dad"

1. After reading the story, why do you think David had a hard time going to school?

2. After reading the story, why did David decide to try harder in school?

3. Why did his Dad buy round-trip tickets?

4. What is different about the city where David's father worked and where they lived?

5. What time do you think David and his father went to work? Why?

6. What do you think it was that caused David to fall asleep on the way home?

7. What advice would you give David knowing how he feels about school and what he wants to be?

8. Rewrite these words and add an ending to them. Try different endings instead of using all the same ones.

shop	_____	pop	_____	want	_____
enter	_____	dance	_____	leave	_____
play	_____	ask	_____	hard	_____
buy	_____	watch	_____	decide	_____
exclaim	_____	tour	_____	whistle	_____
walk	_____	exit	_____	share	_____
chug	_____	gentle	_____	climb	_____
smile	_____	open	_____	reply	_____

9. **This story is mainly about**

___ the train ride.

___ David wanting to be an architect.

___ going to work with Dad.

___ taxis, trains, buildings and stores.

WRITING PROMPT: Write about going to work with your Dad or Mom or someone you care about. Where do they work? How did you get there? What did you do while you were there? What did you like best about it?

"Wannabe"

Russell is the most fun and most popular person I know. Everyone in our neighborhood wants to be with Russell. When we choose teams to play baseball, Russell is always chosen first, and not just baseball, but all team sports. He is exceptional at everything he does. I could go on and on about all the wonderful things that Russell can do, but it just makes me feel stupid, klutzy and dumb.

I just "wannabe" like Russell, then everybody would gather around me and want me to be on their team or be their partner.

I walked home from school by myself, as usual. As I walked, I thought and thought. I knew if I thought long enough and hard enough, I might come up with a fool-proof master plan.

The next morning, I carefully selected what clothes to wear. I tried picking out clothes just like Russell's or one closest to Russell's. Russell always wore sweatshirts, so I borrowed my big sister's green sweatshirt. Green is not one of my favorite colors, but it's the only sweatshirt that I could find to use. I'll have a better selection tomorrow after mom does the washing. I wore my brother's

sneakers, even though my feet are somewhat larger that his. I parted my hair down the middle like Russell's, ate a quick breakfast and took off for school.

Nothing unusual happened at school. No one commented

on how I looked. The sleeves of the sweatshirt kept falling down over my hands and by lunchtime my feet hurt. I hobbled to lunch in the cafeteria. Jake and Daniel sat with Russell to eat. They laughed and enjoyed themselves as usual. I sat by myself and watched to see if I could get a clue as to what I was doing wrong. Whatever was happening with them , I wanted to happen to me.

That night, I thought and thought some more. Finally, I came up with an alternative plan of action. This plan had to work!

The next day, I went to school again dressed as close

to Russell as I could. I watched Russell's every move and tried to mimic everything he did and said, but the neatest thing happened! We had a great art project. We were trying to show perspective in our drawings. It was a blast! I love to draw! Russell was struggling with his. That's when he commented on what a great job I was doing! I offered to help him with his. I just gave him a few suggestions here and a few suggestions there. Russell said that I sure knew a lot about art and that when he needed help, he knew just who to ask!

That night, I walked home with Russell and his friends. We waved good-bye and said we'd see each other later. Russell asked me what I was going to wear tomorrow. I said that I was going to wear my favorite blue sweater and my old clunky, comfortable shoes.

You'll never believe it, but the next day Russell was wearing an old faded blue sweater and had his hair combed like mine! I decided that I "wannabe" just me and that we didn't need two Russell's, even though there are still things about Russel that I admire and "wannabe" like.

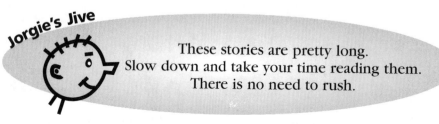

Jorgie's Jive

These stories are pretty long. Slow down and take your time reading them. There is no need to rush.

Follow-up Activities for "Wannabe?"

1. **Use the following words to fill in the blanks: comfortable, exceptional, commented, selection, hobbled, neighborhood, suggestions, alternative, perspective, discouraged.**

   A. I used an _____ plan when the first one didn't work.

   B. I get _____ when I feel klutzy and dumb.

   C. After mom washes, I'll have a better _____.

   D. No one _____ on how I fixed by hair.

   E. I _____ along because my shoes were too small.

   F. In art, when you show depth it means showing _____.

   G. Sometimes a few _____ can help others.

   H. Sloppy clothes are usually _____.

   I. Our _____ is a good place to be.

   J. An outstanding person is an _____ person.

2. **Unscramble these feeling or character words. Sometimes the first letter in the word is underlined for you.**

iswe	_____	lcreev	_____	termyoussi	_____
pyaph	_____	dsa	_____	nmae	_____
iofhsol	_____	nidk	_____	etgsarn	_____
etgsarn	_____	elruc	_____	ynfun	_____
yerfdnil	_____	eayksn	_____	enegosur	_____

3. **Homographs: Write two definitions for the following words: pound, stamp, tire, ring, cold, trip, duck, fly, punch, wave, rock, saw.**

WRITING PROMPT: Write about who you would "wannabe" like and why. Then write about why someone would like to be like you!

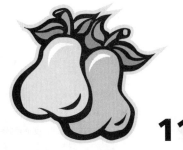

11

Time & Place

School is

> a place for friends to meet.
>
> a place to read and learn new things.
>
> a place for fire drills and recess.
>
> a place for kids to run and play.
>
> a place for experimenting in science.
>
> a place to study customs and cultures.
>
> a place to say the *Pledge of Allegiance*.

Summer is

> a time of warm sunny skies.
>
> a time of water fights and swimming pools.
>
> a time of riding bikes and playing ball.
>
> a time of watching growing things.
>
> a time of mowing grass and picking flowers.
>
> a time for soccer and picnics
>
> a time for vacations with family.
>
> a time for fishing with grandparents.

Fall is

> a time for harvesting on a farm.
>
> a time for preparation for a long winter.
>
> a time of colorful changes of wonder.
>
> a time of baby animals growing up.
>
> a time for football to begin.
>
> a time for school shopping.
>
> a time where summer ends and school begins.

Home is

> a place for parents, children and pets.
>
> a place for food and shelter.
>
> a place of reading and homework.
>
> a place of love and laughter.
>
> a place of tears and sharing.
>
> a place where hugs and kisses are special.
>
> a place to give and receive help.
>
> a place for family and friends.

The world is a place for all this and more,

The world is a place for me!

After reading the poem do the following:

1. **Put these words in alphabetical order:** friends, fire drills, recess, science, report cards, customs, cultures, swimming, flowers, grandparents, soccer, picnics, animals, football.

1.	2.	3.	4.	5.
6.	7.	8.	9.	10.
11.	12.	13.	14.	

2. **Write the opposites for:**

sunny _____   discussing _____

growing _____   vacation _____

prepare _____   harvest _____

grandparents _____   changes _____

winter _____   receive _____

3. **Writing Prompt: Write a word or sentence to complete the following:**

School is _____

Summer is _____

Fall is _____

Spring is _____

Winter is _____

School is _____

Home is _____

Moving to the Big Apple

When Theresa arrived home from school, she found her mom and dad waiting for her in the living room. It was unusual for her parents to be home at such an early hour. Curious, she walked slowly into the living room and sat on the couch next to her mother.

"Theresa, your father was offered a new job with a company in New Your City," her mother said. Theresa didn't respond and there was a long pause before her dad said, "Your mother and I have given it some thought and I'm going to accept the job offer tomorrow." Then, he explained that the company needed him to start work as soon as possible. Theresa asked if this meant they would have to move to New York to which her father replied, "Yes, won't that be exciting!"

Theresa was born in Denver, Colorado and had spent her whole life in the same house. She had many friends in the neighborhood and at school and didn't like the idea of moving so far away from them. She didn't know anything about New York City except from what she had seen on TV. The idea of moving to such a big city and having to make new friends frightened her.

"It's not fair and I'm not moving," she said crying as she ran up the stairs to her room, slamming the door behind her and flopping face-down on the bed. Thoughts of running away crossed her mind. These thoughts just made her angrier and angrier.

Later, she heard a knock on the door.

"Theresa," she heard her mom say. "Jennifer is here and she wants to talk to you." Theresa jumped off the bed and opened the door to see her best friend Jennifer standing there smiling. She wiped the tears from her eyes and told Jennifer to come in, scowling at her mother as she closed the bedroom door.

"My parents told me you're moving to New York City. They said I can come visit you when school lets out," said her friend happily. "I can stay for the whole summer if you want," continued Jennifer. Theresa felt a little better knowing that Jennifer would visit soon and would always be her friend but the idea of leaving still upset her. Jennifer explained that her grandmother lived in New York. She called it the Big Apple. She said she had visited there before and began telling Theresa stories about her many adventures. Little by little, Theresa felt better about the move.

That night, Jennifer stayed for dinner. Theresa's mom made a special cake and they sat around the table swapping stories about what it must be like to live in the Big Apple.

Jorgie's Jive

How are you doing?
Are you using the Incentive Calendar?
Incentives are great motivation!

14

Follow-Up Activities For "Moving to the Big Apple"

1. **Write the reasons why Theresa's father might have accepted the new job offer.**

2. **Write three reasons why Theresa did not want to move.**

3. **Write three reasons why Jennifer came over to see Theresa.**

4. **Cross out the word or words in each row that does not belong with the others.**

A.	crying	pouting	sleeping	shouting	here
B.	curious	interested	inquisitive	upsetting	desire
C.	arrive	came	leave	reach	scramble
D.	hope	reject	wish	respect	scrunch
E.	plan	arrange	order	setup	fore
F.	clear	crush	mash	grind	quarter
G.	forward	backward	front	ahead	
H.	dime	dollar	sent	penny	

5. **Write the correct endings: ed ing ies ip est ures airs ier ers er ily**

   A. Theresa just kept getting angr_____.

   B. She had happ_____ left for school that morning.

   C. She didn't want to hear stor_____ about the Big Apple.

   D. She didn't want to think of the mov_____ that were coming.

   E. Theresa ran up the st_____ to her room.

   F. Jennifer did her b_____ to make her feel better.

   G. She plans on stay_____ the whole summ_____.

   H. They talked about her many advent_____.

   I. Jennifer and Theresa wanted to keep their friendsh_____ forever.

WRITING PROMPT: Pretend that you are moving to a far away country. What will happen? Where will you go? What will you do? How will you get then? What will you do to make yourself happy?

Grandpa Remembers

My Grandpa Yancy lives just down the lane and around the corner from us. I love to go to his house and be with him. He's the one that taught me how to fish and how to play checkers.

In the wintertime, we sit by the fire, eat apples and play games. In the summertime we usually go for a walk. Sometimes, we walk down to the corner market to buy a treat or two. Other times, if I'm lucky, Grandpa is in his "remembering" mood and I'll sit next to him, quietly saying, "Grandpa, tell me one of the 'old time' stories."

"One nippy winter's day, when Phillip wasn't much older than you," grandpa began, "he begged to go with us to harvest a crop of ice- blocks. We got the tractor and wagon hooked up, loaded the equipment, climbed aboard and took off. We went down to the river. When we got there, Ralph tested the ice and said that he'd found an excellent stretch of ice." "It's a good three feet thick out here!" he yelled. "Sounds like it's just right for the taking!" I yelled back.

Samuel broke a large triangular piece of ice into small chunks so that we could handle the ice adequately. I took our "logging" saw down to the river. A logging saw is a long saw with handles at each end, so two people can take hold and take turns pushing and pulling.

Phillip understood how a logging saw worked on a tree but he wanted to know how it worked on cutting ice-blocks. Kiddingly, Samuel told him that one guy has to get down in the water and push, while the guy on top has to pull. At first, Phillip really believed him. It took him a couple of minutes to think about it, and realized that a person would freeze, drown or hyperventilate if he or she had to be in the icy water for more that a few seconds.

Curiosity got the best of him. He stood and watched as the men put the saws in the water. Pushing and pulling on the one end, they cut long slabs of ice. Next they moved the slabs up to the bank and flipped them out. The guys on the bank cut them into square blocks. After the blocks were made, they took the large ice tongs, hooking them into the blocks and put them on the wagon. After the wagon had all the ice blocks it would hold, we headed back to the ice shed.

The ice shed had three or four inches of sawdust on the floor. We put the blocks on top of the sawdust, leaving spaces in-between each block, where we packed more sawdust around the blocks. We kept doing this until we had filled the shed with ice, making sure that there was sufficient sawdust on and around each ice block.

This all took several days and several trips. The most amazing thing about this whole operation was that the ice would last us all summer! Grandpa finished his story by saying, "We always had plenty of delicious home-made ice-cream and cookies all summer!" Sounds like magic to me! I love Grandpa's "remembering" stories!

Jorgie's Jive

Does your Grandpa or Grandma have an interesting story to tell? Ask them. Then write a story about it in your Summer Notes or Journal Page.

Follow-Up Activities for "Grandpa Remembers"

1. Put the following in sequence using numbers:

_____We used the ice tongs to load the wagon;.

_____We loaded the equipment and climbed aboard.

_____Samuel broke a large triangular piece of ice.

_____We hauled the blocks of ice back to the ice shed.

_____Ralph tested the ice.

_____The men used the logging saws to cut the ice.

_____This whole operation would take several days.

2. Prefixes are added to the beginning of a word. tri means three, un means after, pre and pro means before, post means after, re means back or again, dis means appo site, by means near or aside.

Use these prefixes and make new words that make sense.

_____soak	_____angle	_____lock	_____cycle
_____usual	_____do	_____claim	_____card
_____gram	_____courage	_____hole	_____count
_____pone	_____create	_____zip	_____pass
_____side	_____trude	_____sent	_____make
_____cord	_____agree	_____wanted	_____way

3. Complete the sentences with I or me:

A. _____ have t áo do my chores each day.

B. The school bus drops _____ off at school.

C. My sister and _____ have to ride a long way.

D. Everyday _____ have homework to do.

E. My Mother and Dad usually help _____ finish it.

F. My sister gives _____a hug when I do it right.

4. Complete the sentences using contractions.

A. _____ afraid of the dark, so we have a night light.

B. Mark says _____ meet us after school.

C. _____ skipping words when you read.

D. _____ usually the second one to finish everything.

E. Everyone says _____ the smartest girl in class.

F. _____ got ten minutes before you have to go to bed.

G. _____ go home to my cousin's house.

H. Everyone said, "_____ get it over with."

WRITING PROMPT: Interview one of your grandparents and have them help you write a "Remembering Story". If you can't get a grandparent, have your Mom or Dad tell you something they did when they were your age!

Trapped Beneath

My older brother, Paul, and I loved to explore the ocean. We had scuba diving gear. We would go out in the boat off the coast of Maine and set the lobster traps with our father. After that was done, we'd beg him to let us go diving. He'd consent as long as we would take a small lobster basket with us to catch lobsters, in case we saw any. His last words for us this particular day were to stay together and to keep track of how much air we had left in our tanks.

Everything went along as usual until we came upon this old wrecked ship at the bottom of the ocean. I don't know how long it had been there but it must have been there for some time. It was hard to see very well because of all the ocean plants that clung to its side. We were in the process of seeing what we could see, when we noticed some movement by the gaping hole on the front of the ship. Apparently, a group of lobsters had made their home there.

We frantically started scooping up lobsters and putting them in our basket! We swam to the surface and delivered our catch, got another basket and went down for more. We were busy trying to catch the allusive lobsters when I noticed several in the other hole. I thought Paul had seen me as I ducked into it. I scampered after the lobsters! I caught two of them when something startled me! The quick movement stirred up the ocean sand. I became disoriented. I swam in the direction that I thought I should go. Nothing looked familiar. I panicked as I began searching for a way out. In my thrashing around, I caught myself on something on the side of the ship. I was tangled in such a way that I couldn't reach up and free myself. I was so scared that I could hardly breathe. I knew that I was in serious trouble unless Paul could find me and help!

In the meantime, Paul noticed that the oxygen in his tank was getting low! He was concerned that we would both run out of oxygen! He knew that if he was low on oxygen, so was I! He swam all around looking for me, flashing the bright beam of his flashlight on the wrecked ship!

I noticed his light go by! I hammered on the side of the ship to get Paul's attention. He came back and found the hole that I had entered and easily unhooked me!

We surfaced together just as the oxygen in my tank had completely run out! Paul's had run out just seconds before! I exclaimed to dad how Paul had saved my life! Paul said that he had been really scared, but that he would not, could not leave without me. Dad said that we were extremely fortunate and that we needed to be more careful next time. Paul had remembered dad's earlier advice, "Stay together and check on the oxygen level in your tanks". Thank goodness he did, because I hadn't!

Jorgie's Jive

Have you ever written a short story of your own? Take a few minutes and write down a few story ideas.

Follow-Up Activities for "Trapped Beneath"

1. Reread the story and write the words that means the same as:

cage	_____	permission	_____
damage	_____	cling	_____
obvious	_____	transfer	_____
alluded	_____	attention	_____
playfully	_____	worried	_____

2. What was the most important advice the boys received?

3. Why do you think they were supposed to catch lobsters?

4. Rewrite these verbs in the past tense:

enjoy	_____	sweep	_____
stretch	_____	send	_____
throw	_____	push	_____
dust	_____	pull	_____
touch	_____	know	_____
sit	_____	leave	_____
catch	_____	hug	_____
pour	_____	speak	_____
swim	_____	keep	_____
imagine	_____	slide	_____
speak	_____	join	_____
demand	_____	fight	_____
build	_____	touch	_____
pour	_____	think	_____
write	_____	carry	_____

5. Finish the sentences:

A. It was as sour as a _____.

B. He was as lonely as _____.

C. She felt as mean as _____.

D. It was as strange as _____.

E. I'm as funny as a _____.

WRITING PROMPT: Pretend you are scuba diving in the ocean. Describe in detail what you see and what you did! What happened? Who was with you? What advice would you give other scuba divers?

The New Kid

Max was the new kid at Sunnyvale Elementary School. It wasn't long after his first week there that he began to feel right at home. He was never made to feel unwelcome and within a few days of his arrival, he had made several close friend, who showed him around and included him in their after school fun. Fitting in had never been difficult for Max. He made good grades, did well at sports and was generally looked upon with respect by others his age. Sunnyvale was no different.

Like most schools, Sunnyvale held an athletic competition every year called Field Day for all the students. It lasted all day. Students could sign up for as many different events as they wanted. Max signed up for almost all the events: the fifty and the four-hundred meter dash, the high jump, broad jump and the shot put. His friend Buddy signed up for the same events. Buddy had been especially nice to Max when he first arrived. The two boys did almost everything together.

At the end of the day with only one event left, the four-hundred meter dash, Buddy came up to Max and said, "Max, you've won ribbons in almost all the events, I haven't won anything. Would you let me win just this last race?" Max didn't think there was any harm in hanging back a little so his friend could win, so he did. When the group of racers rounded the final corner and headed down the last stretch for the finish line, Buddy was too far behind the pack to place first, second or third. Seeing this, Max started running faster. Giving it all the strength and energy he had, he quickly passed Buddy and the rest of the runners, crossing the finish line just in time to take first place!

When Buddy finished the race, he jogged up to Max and said, "Hey, you promised to let me win." Max explained to his friend, that he thought Buddy was too far behind to place. "I figured it was better for one of us to win than for neither of us," said Max. "Here, it's yours. I want you to have it," he said, handing the ribbon to Buddy. Buddy smiled at Max's offer, but paused before taking the ribbon.

"No, you keep it Max. You won it fair and square. Maybe tomorrow we could practice sprints and next year I"ll win something," said Buddy.

At that moment, Max knew that he and Buddy would always be friends! "Come on," said Max, placing his arm around Buddy's shoulder. "Let's get an ice-cream cone!"

Jorgie's Jive

It can be hard to be the "new kid on the block." Is there somebody new in your neighborhood. If so, introduce yourself, you'll may make their day.

Follow-Up Activities for "The New Kid"

1. What do you think are Max's most important attributes or characteristics.

2. How do you think Buddy felt in this story before and after the race? Why?

3. What other events do you think they had or should have had for Field Day?

4. What advice do you have for Buddy? Why?

5. **Add another word to the words below to make compound words:**

grave	_____	light	_____
ditch	_____	finger	_____
grass	_____	report	_____
some	_____	care	_____
wind	_____	shoe	_____
water	_____	house	_____
mail	_____	down	_____
grape	_____	note	_____
bath	_____	door	_____
black	_____	clothes	_____
foot	_____	rain	_____
night	_____	back	_____
bird	_____	pea	_____
post	_____	sand	_____
super	_____	any	_____
book	_____	star	_____

WRITING PROMPT: Write about what happens during Field Day or Sports Day at your school. Or write about an event that you like at your school. What you usually do and how it turns out. How do you feel about it? Would you prefer things to be different? If so how, what and why?

21

Heroes

Don't tell me I can't, 'cause I can.

Don't tell me to hum, when I sing.

Don't tell me to whisper, I can't.

Help me to smile, when I'm sad.

Teach me to soar and to fly.

Help me to try and I will.

Failures are successes not tried.

Teach me to do my best,

recognize that it is.

Help me to become all I want to be.

Help me, teach me, guide me,

and I will!

After reading the poem do the following:

1. Add "ing" to these words for the poem:

   stop _____   make _____

   treat_____   come _____

2. Write the homonym for "son."   _____

3. Write the pairs of words that rhyme in this poem.

   _____

   _____

4. Have you ever had a lemonade stand? If so tell about it. If not, pretend you are going to have one. Tell about how you can get started. How much you would charge for the lemonade and how it turned out.

SUMMER NOTES:

Write a short story about a fun, interesting or exciting thing you have done this summer.

Can't think of anything? Here's an idea. Go to the library and check out books about your favorite subject.

Skipping Rocks

I'm sure you have heard of skipping rope and skipping feet, but have you ever heard of skipping rocks? My mother was telling me that when she and her brothers and sisters were little, they used to go down by the lake and skip rocks. She said, "The trick to skipping rocks is getting just the right kind of rocks to throw so it will skip over the top of the water two or three times before it sinks."

"I love my mom!"

I had never heard of such a thing. I had always been told that the rocks were heavier than water and would sink. Have you ever seen rocks that float? Me neither, but if my mom says that you can skip rocks, I believe her!

When I went outside, I took more notice of the rocks I stepped on. I tried to envision which ones could skip and which ones would sink. My friend, Brian, wanted to know just what was so wonderful about rocks that would capture all my attention. I tried to explain that I was looking for rocks that skipped. It took me a while to help him understand what I meant. He said, "I want to see these marvelous skipping rocks in action!" We went inside my house so that my mom could verify my story. I knew that Brian thought I was a little crazy, or maybe a whole lot crazy!

The next afternoon, my mom invited Brian to go with us to the park. Mom and I had our pockets full of "skipping" rocks. They were the flattest rocks we could find and not too big either.

We arrived at the park and went directly to the pond. We found a spot away from people and ducks. Mom proceeded to show us how to hold the rocks just so and with a flick of the wrist, to hurl them into the air, not too high and not too low.

The first couple of times, it didn't work. She said, "I'm just out of practice. I haven't done this for a long time. Be patient, believe me it will work." Finally, she got the hang of it and was soon skipping rocks across the pond!

Brian and I practiced and practiced. "It's kind of like throwing a frisbee," I said. We just about had it, when we ran out of rocks. Mom sat in the shade while we went on a scavenger hunt for more.

With our pockets stuffed with rocks, we ran back to the lake. Believe it or not, before we left the lake, we had those "skipping" rocks skimming the water once, twice and even three times! "What a great sport," we cheered.

Jorgie's Jive

Remember, there are a lot of good books to read on the "Summer Reading List." The more you read, the better reader you will be!

24

Follow-Up Activities for "Skipping Rocks"

1. **What other sports can you think of that you wouldn't need to pay for equipment besides "Skipping Rocks"?**

2. **Read the words in each group. Place them in sequence to make a complete thought.**

___ seen skipping
___ have you ever
___ rocks that float

___ a snail moves
___ through the grass
___ ever so slowly

___ how to do all
___ parents know
___ kinds of fun things

___ to fly, zip and soar
___ butterflies like
___ among the flowers and sky

___ sandwiches and pop
___ it's not a
___ picnic without

___ sort of like
___ throwing a frisbee
___ skipping rocks is

___ in the park
___ run and play
___ children like to

___ sometimes you
___ just have to try
___ over and over again

___ friends come over
___ fun when my
___ I always have

___ have you ever
___ with the ducks
___ swam in a pond

3. **These are possessive pronouns: yours, mine, my, its, ours, his, hers, theirs, their, her, our, your. Write a least six sentences using possessive pronouns.**

WRITING PROMPT: Invent a new game using rocks. You could choose an old game and give it a new twist using rocks. What are the rules and how do you play it? Is it a team sport or a "one on one" game?

The County Fair

I love to go to the county fair,

The noises and smells are uniquely theirs.

The people, the animals, the food,

All create a wonderful mood.

You can hear the animals in the shed,

Calling loudly to their owners to be fed.

The county fair barkers holler, "come play",

"You've only got such a short time to stay."

The rides, oh the rides, are so exciting,

On top of the ferris wheel you see all the lighting.

Mom always ask if we need a lunch,

No way, we want carnie dogs to munch.

Yes, hot dogs, drinks and cotton candy,

Are a must for me and my family.

I love to go to the county fair,

The fun, excitement is abundantly there!

After reading the poem answer the following questions.

1. Write three things that were listed in the County Fair.

2. List some things that you like that were not mentioned.

3. What is it talking about when it said county fair barkers?

4. Write a synonym for abundantly._____

5. Write an antonym for abundantly._____

Visiting Dr. White

On a snowy school day last winter, my little sister slipped and fell on our driveway. I was the first to find her crying and holding her leg. I wasn't sure what was wrong, but I immediately ran inside the house and told mom. Mom went outside and picked my sister up off the ground, took a look at her leg and said, "We better get you to the hospital." I don't know who was more frightened, me or my sister. I almost started to cry, but mom put her arm around me and said everything would be okay.

We drove to the emergency entrance of the hospital and someone came out with a wheelchair for my sister. Mom and I parked the car and stepped into the reception area to wait. My sister was wheeled into another room that was hidden behind a large blue curtain. I sat and watched doctors and nurses run back and forth while my mom filled out lots of forms. After what seemed like hours, a doctor came into the reception area and said, "Hi, my name is Dr. White." I thought that was funny because he was dressed in a white coat. I couldn't help but smile, but I covered my mouth so he wouldn't see. "Would you like to come with your mother into the examination room to see your sister?" he asked me. I nodded and we followed Dr. White past the blue curtain and into a brightly lit room with all kinds of machines and shiny objects.

My sister was sitting on a bed with wheels on it. She had stopped crying and looked much better. Dr. White removed an ice pack from my sister's leg and pointed to a purple bruise around her ankle. He explained that she had sprained her ankle and that she would have to keep it wrapped up for four to six weeks to allow it to heal. My sister winced a little in pain as the doctor brought her leg closer for my mom to take a look. "It will probably be a little sore for a while and she should try to keep from walking on it," he said. Looking at me he asked, "Do you think you could help your sister with things for a week so she doesn't have to walk around too much on her ankle?" I told him I would try. He gave me and my sister some stickers and candy.

It didn't take long for my sister's ankle to heal. She now runs around on it, like nothing ever happened. We visited Dr. White once more for what he called a "follow-up" visit to make sure my sister's ankle was okay. The second visit wasn't nearly as scary as the first. I think I like doctors.

Follow-Up Activities for "Visiting Dr. White"

1. **Word referents in sentences can stand for other words. Read each sentence, then circle the word that the <u>underlined</u> word stands for.**

    A.   Juanita likes to run. <u>It</u> is good for her.
    B.   The black dog ran after the boy. <u>He</u> barked and barked.
    C.   My little sister hurt <u>her</u> leg on the sidewalk.
    D.   Sam and Sara painted today. <u>Their</u> pictures were very good.
    E.   Frank said that <u>his</u> grandfather loves to fish.
    F.   Mark has a fence around his yard. <u>It</u> is six feet high.
    G.   Myra and Skip are friends. <u>They</u> do everything together.
    H.   Dr. White is a careful doctor. <u>He</u> also smiles a lot.
    I.   Robert and Zelma read a lot. "<u>We</u> are good readers," they say.
    J.   The sun is very important. <u>It</u> helps things grow.

2. **Write down how many syllables are in each word.**

    snowy _____   area _____   asked _____   winter _____
    reception _____   leg _____   find _____   ankle _____
    better _____   another _____   heal _____   emergency_____
    stopped _____   removed _____   immediately _____   doctors _____
    brought _____   white _____   winced _____
    examination _____   hospital_____   nurses _____
    probably _____   around _____   sister _____
    explained _____   slipped _____

3. **Use ph, pl, or pr to complete these words:**

    _____ace   _____esent   _____ato   _____rase
    _____oblem   _____antom   _____anets   _____ot
    _____ize   go_____er   re_____y   _____ove
    tro_____y   sur_____ise   sup_____y   ne_____ew
    geogra_____y   air_____ane   a_____on   ap_____oach
    telegra_____   autogra_____   com_____ain   im_____ove
    ap_____y   im_____ession   ex_____ess   per_____ex
    trium_____

WRITING PROMPT: Have you or someone you know, ever have to go to the hospital or to the doctor? Write about your experience. What happened that caused you to have to go? Who went with you? What did the doctor have to do? How did you feel about the experience?

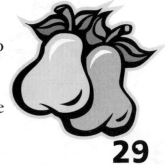

29

What's That Noise

We found what looked like the opening to a natural cave and went inside. We could see four or five feet ahead of us, but beyond that it was too dark to see anything. Neither of us had thought to bring flashlights. Though we wanted to discover how deep the cave was, we decided it would be too dangerous to go further without them. We had heard stories of kids getting caught under falling rocks and other debris inside caves that collapsed, also stories of people falling down old mine shafts in the cave floor. Though eager to explore the whole cave, especially before any of our other friends discovered it, we thought better to make a mental note and bring flashlights next time.

What could be seen in the cave was fascinating enough, for the time being, anyway. The floor was dry and sandy, but firm. The walls were bumpy and irregularly shaped in dull, gray rock. Veins of another, shinier substance could be seen in the wall, glistening in the light like little rivers trapped between looming valleys and mountains. It was a wonderful sight!

Inside the cave it was nice and shady, so we decided to take a break from the hot sun and sit, while enjoying our lunch. There were a couple of large rocks on the floor that were perfect for sitting on. They were placed near each other and I wondered if someone else had been here before us. We emptied our knapsacks of their contents: two canteens, two tunafish sandwiches, an orange and a candy bar. After unwrapping and enjoying our sandwiches, I leaned back against the cave wall and closed my eyes, while my friend busied himself with the orange. It sounded as if a breeze had picked up outside the cave. I listened to it, feeling very relaxed. In my hand, I fondled a rock that I had found, which was made of the shiny substance in the walls. I intended to take it home with me to add to my growing rock collection. It felt cool and heavy in the palm on my hand and strangely soothing.

Suddenly, I heard a shuffling and scratching noise! I opened my eyes to find my friend staring back at me with a questioning look that said, "What's that noise?" We sat still for a while in silence, then we heard more scratching and a muffled moan issued from the dark end of the cave!

"Run," I yelled! Run we did, leaving our knapsacks and what was left of our lunch, behind!

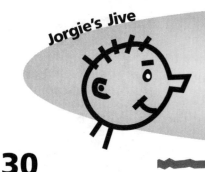

Jorgie's Jive

Remember to have fun while reading these stories.
Be creative. Try changing the end of the stories.
Draw a picture of your new ending.

Name _____

Follow-Up Activities for "What's That Noise"

1. What do you think the "Shinier" substance was that the story talked about? Why?

2. What do you think could have made the shuffling, scratching and moaning sound? Explain your reasoning.

3. Do you think they ever went back to the cave? Why or why not?

4. How old do you think the children in this story are? Why? Do you think that they are boys or girls or both? Why?

5. Write the correct vowel or vowels in the blanks. They must be real words.
   Use these vowels: a e i o u

adm___t	___gly	b___ggar	___ther	st___p
scr___p	s___gnal	adm___t	f___nd	___ncle
wh___p	st___p	pean___t	seas___n	sk___tch
ups___t	gr____duate	b___d	b___g	d___gout
b___nch	___tch	fl___t	bl___t	w___t

Use these vowel pairs in the words below: ea ai oa ie

t_____d	b_____t	sp_____k	b_____ch	d_____l
t_____m	gr_____n	tr_____d	t_____st	n_____l
g_____t	p_____	dr_____m	appr_____ch	d_____sy
f_____m	sn_____l	pl_____se	cr_____k	l_____d
_____d	ch_____p	sp_____d	pl_____d	d_____d

WRITING PROMPT: Write sentences that are the funniest, saddest, longest, shortest, believable, most unbelievable and outrageous.

31

Breakfast

What's for breakfast this morning , I ask,

My mother says it will be a surprise.

She says making breakfast is such a task,

Having orange juice and a muffin is wise.

How about eggs and bacon with fruit and cereal,

Don't think about pizza and cake.

Toast and eggs make the day seem real,

Starting with breakfast is always great.

Okay, I say, make my eggs scrambled,

I don't want them sunny-side up.

My hot chocolates too hot to be handled,

Put lots of milk in my cup.

My dad says to unscramble his eggs,

How I wonder, when it's already done.

I think dad is just pulling our legs,

He eats his eggs on a hamburger bun.

We're out the door, we're on our way,

Here comes the bus.

Mom shouts "Have a good day".

and with my breakfast inside me, I shout back, "Okay!"

After reading the poem, do the following:

1. **Put the following in sequence as listed in the poem using numbers.**

   _____scrambled eggs   _____pizza   _____orange juice

   _____milk   _____hamburger bun   _____muffin

   _____unscrambled eggs   _____fruit   _____hot chocolate

   _____ toast

2. **Write a list of nutritious things that you should have for breakfast.**

3. **Write a list of unhealthy foods that you should not have for breakfast.**

Sweet Porridge

A Fairy Tale

There was a poor but good little girl who lived alone with her mother. They no longer had anything to eat. The child went into the forest to see if she could find some wild blueberries to bring home.

While she was looking for some berries, she saw an old woman. The woman was bent and straggled with stringy, long, gray hair and sparse, yellow teeth. The little girl felt sorry for the old woman and gave her all of the meager berries that she had found.

The old woman was actually an enchanted forest witch and was charmed by the young girl's kindness. For her generosity, the witch gave her a magic pot. She said, "Remember these words and you will never be hungry again, cook, little pot, cook. It will cook good sweet porridge. When you say, stop, little pot, stop, it will cease to cook."

The girl took the pot home to her mother. Now they were no longer hungry, but ate sweet porridge whenever they chose.

One time when the girl had gone out to wander in the forest to thank the old woman for the great gift, her mother decided to make some porridge. She said, "Cook, little pot, cook," and it did cook. She ate till she was satisfied and then she wanted the pot to stop cooking. She forgot the words! So it went on cooking and cooking. The porridge rose over the edge. Still it cooked on until the kitchen and the whole house were full. It then filled the next house and the next, and then the whole street, just as if it wanted to satisfy the hunger of the whole world.

There was the greatest distress! People were running away from their homes, taking what they could carry. No one knew how to stop the cooking pot. Everyone feared for their lives!

When only one single house remained, the child heard the torment ringing from the town. She ran till she thought her heart would burst and saw a most horrible sight. She scurried to her home and said, "Stop, little pot, stop!" It stopped and gave up cooking. Whosoever wished to return to the town had to eat his way back.

Jorgie's Jive

Slow and steady is the key to acquiring good reading skills.
Keep up the good work, you're almost finished!

Follow-Up Activities for "Sweet Porridge"

1. Write a summary in complete sentences, telling in order the events that happened in the story.

2. In complete sentences, describe how the problems were solved in this fairy tale.

3. What other kinds of problems could have happened when the pot kept cooking and cooking?

4. Find the word distress in the story. Can you figure out the meaning of this word by reading it and how it relates to the other words? How? Why?

5. Write the silent letters that are missing.

wou___d	___rite	cou___d	___now
bac___	throu_____	ri_____t	ans___er
shou___d	hi_____	li_____t	thou_____t
mi_____t	oft___n	ni_____t	wa___k
en___ugh	wa___ch	ta___k	___new

WRITING PROMPT: A Fairy Tale is what we call "make-believe". Use the same type of information but write a story using pop-corn instead of porridge. Make as realistic as possible even though it is a fairy

Neighborhood Reporters

A bunch of us kids decided that we wanted to be newspaper and television reporters when we grew up. "Why wait?" said Benson. "Yeh, why wait?" chimed in Tyler. "What could we report about and what would we do?" I inquired. "Well, let's get organized," we all exclaimed!

"We could use my treehouse for our headquarters," volunteered Jiffy. "I've got some great binoculars that we can use when we're in our headquarters! We can use them to look around to observe what's going on!" Janna shouted. "My dad has a laptop computer that he rarely uses." said Tess, "Maybe he'll let us use it! This is great guys! Let's all go and get what we need and meet back at Jiffy's treehouse in an hour," we all said in unison!

We all scampered off in our different directions, each seeking materials and equipment that we might use. We arrived at Jiffy's treehouse loaded with all kinds of things. We assembled them all together and took inventory of what we had. We had pencils, notebooks, clipboards, pens, binoculars and a laptop computer!

We started discussing topics that we might want to report. Janna was looking

through her binoculars when she said, "Looks like little Georgie Willows is having a problem of some kind." He was sitting on his front steps , just crying and crying. "You guys keep up the discussion while I go see what's wrong with Georgie," Pete said.

Pretty soon Pete was back and wanted us to help him. Georgie's hamster got loose in his yard and he can't find him anywhere. We all left what we were doing and went to help. We looked everywhere and were just about to give up, when we heard the dog next door barking, excitedly.

We went over to see if the dog knew something that we didn't. He had trapped that poor, scared little hamster in the garage. We rescued the frightened little guy and took him back to Georgie. Georgie was thrilled! He promised to take better care of him.

We left and went back to the treehouse. "Well we could write a report about Georgie and his hamster," laughed Alex.

Several of us laughed and agreed. "We could follow it up with an article of how to take care of pets," he added.

Jiffy's sister Ruth came up to join us. She wanted to be part of the action. She brought some cookies for us to munch on. She also had her mom's cellular phone. She said she was expecting a phone call and didn't want to miss it.

We were talking, laughing and generally goofing off, when Craig said, "Hey you guys, knock it off and take a look." We soon found out what he was pointing at. Mrs. Stevens was laying in her backyard clutching her chest, then she stopped moving all together. "Ruth, dial 911, I think Mrs. Olson is in trouble!" yelled Craig. "I'll go down and see if I can help!" Pete exclaimed.

Pete and I got down and ran into Mrs. Stevens' backyard! She was not moving! I ran after my mom! She came and started CPR on Mrs. Stevens. Soon the ambulance arrived! They took her to the hospital!

She had suffered a heart attack! Quick thinking by the "Neighborhood Reporters" had saved her life! After that we became known as the "Neighborhood Watch" alias the "Neighborhood Reporters!"

Jorgie's Jive
Are you reading these stories several times?
Trust me, it's a good idea to do this.
It's great practice for great readers!

Follow-Up Activities for "Neighborhood Reporters"

1. **Put these events that happened in sequential order using numbers.**

___ The children used Jiffy's treehouse for their headquarters.
___ A group of kids that wanted to be reporters got together.
___ Ruth brought her mother's cellular phone while she wanted to be part of the action.
___ They got what they thought they needed and met back at headquarters to plan.
___ Quick thinking "neighborhood reporters" became known for saving Mrs. Stevens.
___ They were getting organized when Georgie needed help so they helped him.
___ Mrs. Stevens had a heart attack, they called 911 and went to help.

2. **Choose the correct meaning for each word. You could use the dictionary if you need to.**

A. ___ sudden   1. pick
   ___ finish   2. scarce
   ___ choose   3. chat
   ___ begin   4. quick
   ___ tell   5. grief
   ___ rare   6. plain
   ___ talk   7. end
   ___ sorrow   8. start
   ___ sick   9. ill
   ___ simple   10. say

B. ___ silly   1. below
   ___ answer   2. copy
   ___ under   3. unhappy
   ___ sad   4. intelligent
   ___ finish   5. frighten
   ___ lean   6. tall
   ___ smart   7. complete
   ___ high   8. foolish
   ___ imitate   9. thin
   ___ scare   10. reply

C. ___ true   1. noisy
   ___ trip   2. enemy
   ___ loud   3. real
   ___ foe   4. error
   ___ mistake   5. happy
   ___ neat   6. journey
   ___ rot   7. calm
   ___ relaxed   8. tidy
   ___ cheerful 9. save
   ___ rescue   10. decay

D. ___ jealous   1. save
   ___ keep   2. dull
   ___ rich   3. worship
   ___ adore   4. scowl
   ___ frown   5. instruct
   ___ strange   6. envious
   ___ short   7. cost
   ___ boring   8. wealthy
   ___ teach   9. peculiar
   ___ price   10. brief

WRITING PROMPT: Try to use some of the words listed above, write about something that you plan on doing. Or write about something you have done or would like to do this summer.

37

Our fame had spread after Mrs. Stevens' heart attack. She was so thankful that we had come to her rescue that she donated one of her cellular phones from her home. She offered to pay the phone bill if we used it only for emergencies and only while were we in the tree house. When we were not there, Mrs. Stevens kept it for us. The local merchants donated more binoculars and computer paper. So, we had a nice set up.

We met regularly to discuss what we could do. Some of us would find out who was sick and deliver their groceries. Another thing we did was, if someone was going to be out of town, we'd feed their pet for them. We even did a little baby sitting for people that had to run short errands, while their young children were napping. We always worked in small or large groups when doing volunteer work.

One day we helped Janie when she fell off her bike and skinned both knees, her elbow and chin. Janie was a wreck and so was her bicycle. We helped to get both home safely. After her mom took care of her cuts and bruises, she took a look at the bike. She had us take it down to Janie's Grandpa's shop to get it fixed. Janie's mom offered to pay us for helping but we declined saying, we were just glad that we could help.

Probably the most exciting event happened one Saturday, late in the afternoon. A few of us were up in the treehouse just talking and visiting about nothing in particular. We had just finished playing a soccer game and had gone to the treehouse for a few minutes before returning home. Michael was staring out of the window, when he noticed something that looked rather suspicious.

There was an unmarked blue van pulled up in the Walker's driveway. Three men were loading a television, a VCR, and golf clubs. We knew that the Walker's were out of town for the weekend. Apparently we weren't the only ones! We called 911 and reported what we had seen! They kept us on the line asking questions while they sent some policemen to investigate.

We told them the name and address of the Walker's. We described what the guys looked like and what they were wearing. We also described the blue van and even saw part of the license plate number.

The police told us to stay put, to keep watching but most important to stay out of sight. They told us to be extremely careful and leave the rest to them.

Before the police could get there the guys got in the van and started driving away. They went south on River Street and turned the corner on Short Street. We gave the police the information on the phone and then waited right where we were.

It wasn't long before we heard the police sirens. We watched as the police cars drove past the Walker's house, down River Street and turn on Short Street.

We were told later that the police apprehended the suspects and retrieved all of the Walker's stolen things. Plus, they retrieved several other stolen articles and equipment. These same guys had robbed several other places and were taking the things out of town to pawn shops.

The police called us all heroes and important members of our community. They said because of our "Neighborhood Watch Club" that we had solved a real problem for them. They told us again how great we were! They also said that the most important thing though, was for us to be very careful so that we could remain safe while serving our neighborhood. That we were not to go out looking for crimes to solve but to continue to be available to serve others in need!

We went home feeling really proud of ourselves and our club, knowing that we had made a real difference.

Follow-Up Activities for "Neighborhood Watch"

1. Write down in complete sentences the important facts that the dispatcher at 911 and the police needed that helped apprehend the thieves.

2. What was dangerous about this situation?

3. Read the words on each line. Add another word that would belong in that group.

    1. pants shirt shoes socks _____

    2. soccer baseball racquetball _____

    3. punch milk water _____

    4. bread rolls bagels _____

    5. carrots turnips potatoes _____

    6. oranges apples pears _____

    7. ocean river stream _____

    8. cup saucer bowl _____

    9. shovel hammer hoe _____

    10. eyes chest arms _____

WRITING PROMPT: Write about your neighborhood. Draw a map and label the places on your street. Pretend there's a problem on your street and you have to call 911! What was the problem and what happened?

Riddle Me This

Riddle me this, riddle me that.

Why is a cat not a bat or a rat?

Or a flea not a bee, a shark not a lark?

And why do we say no light means it's dark?

What makes a train not a car or a plane?

And why call it a train come sunshine or rain?

Why not call it a creeper or chugger or super fast, super sleek, big wooly bugger?

Because a train is a train is a train is a train.

It's a train for your sister, your mom and your dad,

A train for Aunt Sue, Uncle Joe, Cousin Brad.

It's a train in Egypt, France and St. Paul,

No matter it's course or what it might haul.

When it leaves the station or rounds the bend,

A train is a train and to this riddle, no end.

We're told it's a train so a train it shall be.

But I'll tell you a secret, just between you and me,

I prefer super fast, super sleek, big wooly bugger!

After reading the poem do the following:

1. Write down the words in the poem that rhyme.

2. Solve these riddles:

What is black and white and "red" all over? _____

What has eyes but cannot see? _____

What has horns but doesn't beep? _____

What kind of bed should you not sleep in? _____

3. Write down a descriptive word or words for train.

4. Write some other reasonable ways to travel.

SUMMER NOTES:

Draw a picture of a fun, interesting or exciting thing you want to do this summer.

Having trouble? Read the newspaper with your mom or dad. Talk about any interesting stories you may find. Have you ever thought about being a newspaper reporter.

A Surprise on a Snowy Saturday

It was early Saturday morning when Chuck's mom woke him from a deep sleep. "Rise and shine. Your father and I have something special in store for you!" she said as she flipped on the lamp switch and sat down on Chuck's bed.

Chuck rubbed his eyes and sat up wondering what the surprise was. His mother told him to get dressed. "Put on a warm sweater, your snow pants and parka. Grab your hat, and gloves. Meet me in the kitchen. We'll have a quick breakfast and then we're all going snow boarding!"

Chuck couldn't believe it. His big brother, who was thirteen, had been snow boarding for five years and raced competitively at the local ski resort every weekend. Chuck had been asking to go with his brother for a long time. His parents said he had to wait until he was eight.

He dressed quickly and bounded down the stairs into the kitchen where his dad, brother and mom were waiting. "You better hustle and eat your breakfast. We have a long day ahead of us and it's snowing," said his dad.

After breakfast, Chuck's brother motioned for Chuck to follow him out to the garage where he kept his snow boarding gear. He handed Chuck a red snow board, a pair of ski goggles and some special boots that he had outgrown years ago. "You'll need these," he said with a grin. Chuck could hardly believe it! His brother always took such good care of his equipment and would never let Chuck use it in

any way shape or form. Now, he was just handing it over to him for good!

Chuck thanked his brother. The whole family piled into the car. Eager to get to the resort, Chuck almost left his hat and gloves behind on the kitchen table. "Make sure you have everything," said his dad as he back the car out of the garage into the street.

The snow was coming down fast and heavy as Chuck's dad maneuvered the car up the mountain road. Chuck had been on this road before, but it was summer then. Everything looked so different. The trees were covered in snow now and icicles hung form their branches. He gazed happily out the car window as the swirling snow landed silently on the mountain tops.

In a short while, they arrived at the base of the mountain, where they bought four tickets for 20 dollars a piece. With his brother's instructions, Chuck loaded the chair lift, which swung in the wind as it moved up the mountain. The two boys huddled for warmth. Chuck winced as the snow hit his face. "Does it hurt?" asked his brother. "No, it tickles," laughed Chuck.

Chuck's parents told the boys they were going to the top of the mountain. They arranged a meeting place and time for lunch. As they rounded the corner out of Chuck's sight, his brother helped him strap onto his board. "I wish I could go to the top of the mountain with mom and dad," said Chuck. "Don't worry, you'll

get there soon enough," said his brother encouragingly.

Chuck stood at the top of the hill watching his brother take five or six turns. It looked easy enough, but Chuck was having trouble balancing. "Come on, you can do it," yelled his brother from below. Chuck closed his eyes and pointed the front of the board downhill. Almost immediately, he caught an edge and fell face down into the snow. He watched as a few kids who looked his age fly by him. He felt a little humiliated but the newly fallen snow was soft and cushioned his fall. He started to laugh and so did his brother, "Even falling is fun," exclaimed Chuck!

By mid-afternoon when Chuck and his brother started for the lunch meeting place, Chuck was linking his turns and could make four or five without falling.

"I'm proud of you," said Chuck's brother, "You're doing great! I think you'll be boarding from the top of the mountain sooner than you think." He added, "You're doing better than I did at your age!" Chuck filled his lungs with a breath of cool mountain air and took off down the last pitch of the ski hill!

"Let's go! Last one down buys lunch," he called back to his brother, who grinned and started after him. He laughed and thought to himself: That's a safe bet cause you know mom and dad are buying lunch.

Follow-Up Activities for "Snow Saturday"

1. Read and then mark the sentences that tell about the story.
- A. ___ Chuck left his hat and gloves behind on the kitchen table.
- B. ___ The lift tickets cost Chuck's family twenty dollars a piece.
- C. ___ The boys met their parents at the top of the mountain.
- D. ___ Chuck had to hurry and eat so that they could go.
- E. ___ The trees had icicles hanging from them and the snow covered the mountain slopes.
- F. ___ Chuck's brother was five years older than him.
- G. ___ They had a lot of fun skiing together down the mountain slopes.
- H. ___ Chuck's brother was very proud of how well he did.
- I. ___ Chuck twisted is ankle when he fell but got right up and took off again.
- J. ___ Chuck and his family were not the only ones up there that day.

2. What happened in the story that makes you think that Chuck had fun?

3. What made him feel somewhat humiliated?

4. This story is mostly about:
- ___ the mountains and snow
- ___ about winter sports
- ___ Chuck and his brother snow boarding

5. What would be another appropriate title for this story?
- ___ A Snowy Day
- ___ Chuck's Big Day
- ___ Snow Landing on Chuck and His Brother

6. Why did Chuck do so well his first day?
- ___ His brother told him to do well.
- ___ Because he already had practiced.
- ___ He didn't give up when he fell.

7. Mark all the things that you think are important when you go snow boarding.
- ___ Know a good place to go.
- ___ When you are first learning, get help from someone who really knows how to do it.
- ___ Go with people you know.
- ___ Don't give up unless you really get hurt or tired.
- ___ Go where it is safe to go.
- ___ Wear your warm clothes.
- ___ Don't forget any of your equipment.
- ___ Have fun and keep improving.

WRITING PROMPT: Write down as many ways that you can possibly think of to compliment, encourage or praise someone. Things like: Way to Go! Fantastic! Wow!

Friday's Swim

It was Friday, the last day of swim practice for the week and Laura wasn't looking forward to it. Friday was the day the coach asked all the swimmers to swim the entire length of the pool without stopping to take a breath. Try as she might, Laura couldn't do it. Every time she hit the halfway mark, she would turn on her side, take one big breath and continue to the end.

Laura knew she was a good swimmer. She had learned a lot during the summer. She could swim much faster than she could last year. She had won ten ribbons already this summer as proof of her hard work: two blue, first-place ribbons; three red, second-place ribbons, and five white, third-place ribbons. As she wiggled into her swimsuit, she surveyed the ribbons, which were spread out and proudly displayed on top of her dresser. Just seeing them made her feel better about going to practice. Maybe I can do it this time," she thought to herself as she left the house.

Practice went well that morning. Laura felt strong and the coach had complimented her on her backstroke. She was having fun doing handstands underwater and splashing around in the shallow end of the pool, when the coach blew his whistle. He asked everyone to get out and line up on the pool's edge at the deep end. Already? said Laura quietly

to herself. She was the last person out of the pool and lagged behind as everyone lined up. Secretly she hoped that they would run out of time before it was her turn to make the swim. Soon enough though, her time came.

The coach pulled her aside. "Laura, I know you can do this." I've seen you work hard this summer. You've become a good little swimmer. There's nothing to be afraid of. Now, give it a try," said the coach with an affectionate grin.

Laura line up, gripping the pool's edge with her toes and readied herself for take-off. The coach gave a whistle and she dove into mid-air, landing in the water with a splash. She went as fast as she could. Her cheeks were bulging with air as if they were going to burst. She could see the halfway mark just ahead, and started kicking furiously. "Come on," she repeated over and over in her mind. Coming up on the halfway mark, she started to feel dizzy and had to really restrain herself from taking a much needed breath. She succeeded in holding on until she got about a two-thirds of the way down the pool, at which point she surfaced for a quick breath and continued.

When she got to the end, the coach was waiting. "Take a short rest and do it again," he said. "I can't," said Laura. The coach helped Laura out of the

pool and walked with her to the deep end. "If you say 'I can't' then you won't," he advised her. "Listen to me, I know you can do it."

Laura decided it wouldn't hurt to give it another try. She lined   up and waited for the whistle. The whistle blew and

she was off like a rocket! She tried not to think about breathing, just focusing on her strokes and kicking. She felt so determined. Sooner than she expected, she passed the halfway mark. Worried that she might lose her concentration, she closed her eyes , counting her strokes in her mind. One, two, three, four, she counted. Before she knew it her right arm hit the side of the pool! She surfaced, took a big breath of air and opened her eyes. There was her coach, grinning from ear to ear!

"You did it!" he said. "Yeah, I guess I did!" she said as she looked back toward the deep end. She thought to herself, Friday's aren't so bad after all!

Follow-Up Activities for "Friday's Swim"

1. **List the things mentioned in the story that made Laura feel good about herself.**

2. **What things in the story tell you about Laura being reluctant to try to swim all the way without taking a breath?**

3. **Why was the coach so determined for Laura to succeed?**

4. **Homonyms are two words that sound alike but are spelled differently. Choose the correct homonym for each word.**

A.				B.			
___ knot	1. our			___ sea	1. whale		
___ rain	2. ail			___ meat	2. flower		
___ ate	3. wore			___ aunt	3. see		
___ break	4. rein			___ wail	4. ant		
___ hour	5. eight			___ road	5. be		
___ ale	6. heal			___ stair	6. meet		
___ sail	7. not			___ sew	7. won		
___ war	8. sale			___ one	8. so		
___ heel	9. here			___ bee	9. rode		
___ hear	10. red			___ flour	10. stare		
___ read	11. brake			___ hymn	11. him		

C.				D.			
___ knew	1. four			___ piece	1. son		
___ for	2. sum			___ great	2. peace		
___ some	3. new			___ threw	3. by		
___ mail	4. blue			___ steel	4. two		
___ beat	5. male			___ sun	5. pale		
___ bare	6. would			___ buy	6. days		
___ blew	7. fur			___ too	7. through		
___ flew	8. beet			___ their	8. right		
___ dents	9. dense			___ write	9. grate		
___ fir	10. flu			___ daze	10. there		
___ wood	11. bear			___ pail	11. steal		

WRITING PROMPT: Write and describe the biggest sandwich you have ever eaten. Go into detail. Use your imagination. You can exaggerate!

45

Oh, Where are We Going

Oh, where are we going?
Oh, where are we going?
No knowing, no knowing.

Under the fence and through the yard,
Come, follow me, it's not so hard.
Over the hill and near the stream,
Is where I go to dare to dream.

By the large tree, under the shade,
Is where we can sit unafraid.
Of being told what's right or wrong,
And make up words to our very own song.

Oh where are we going?
No knowing, no knowing.

We'll sing of a land far away,
Where elves and fairies hide and play.
Or pretend we're pirates at sea,
Seeking adventure, wild and free.
We'll watch the birds high in the sky,

Smell the flowers and wonder why.
The grass is green, and water blue,
We'll figure it out, me and you.

Oh, where are we going?
No knowing , no knowing.

When the light fades and mother calls,
For our return before night falls.
We'll reply with a plea, "More time!"
And up the big tree we'll climb.

To watch the great sun as it sets,
"See, there's still light, we've more time yet."
We'll say, knowing the day is gone,
But certain that not before long,
We'll be back to this place and wonder
together.

Oh where are we going?
No knowing, no knowing.

After reading the poem do the following:

1. **Write the rhyming pairs written in the poem.**

2. **Write a homonym for:**   blue_____   high _____
    you_____   right _____

3. **Write the root word (base word) for:**
    unafraid _____   seeking _____
    pretend _____   return _____
    knowing _____   adventure _____
    pirates _____   being _____

4. **In the poem it talks about some things that are real and some things that are make-believe. What are the things that are considered fiction?**

Name _____

If I Were

Heroes start out as ordinary people,
People like you and like me.
Heroes don't wait for things to happen,
They take advantage of the here and now.

Heroes pick themselves up when they stumble,
They try their best and then they try some more.
Heroes take action when action is called for,
Yet stand back, letting others feel needed.

Heroes take time for kindness and friendships,
Not asking to be first in people's hearts,
But finding themselves there.

Heroes are willing to give their all,
To make the world a better place.

We look to heroes to pattern ourselves after,
Thinking that they are wonderous and great.
Look to yourselves, taking care of the small things,

Working through the hard,
For sometimes unknowingly,
People are looking to us, their hero!

After reading the poem do the following:

1. **Write a list of three of four attributes mentioned in the poem.**

2. **Write three or four additional attributes of heroes that you think are important.**

3. **What does it mean by, "Not asking to be first in people's hearts but finding themselves there?"**

4. **Find the word in the poem that means the opposite of:**

    telling_____   disadvantage _____

    extraordinary_____   front _____

    take _____   playing _____

    unwilling _____   knowing_____

Runaways

Chores, chores, chores. I'm so tired of doing chores. "Take the garbage out." "Pick up your toys." "Watch your little brother." "Help dad in the garden." " Go to the grocery store and get a gallon of milk for me, please." I bet my friends don't have to work so hard. I bet they get to watch all the television they want, probably spending most of their time swimming in the county pool, riding their bicycles and playing games.

When I get older, I'm not going to do any of these things. I was out in our yard grumbling, when my friend, Dennis came by. "Where are you going?" I asked him. He said that he had to help his brother deliver newspapers because his brother had gone to a birthday party. "Bummer," I said. We both were complaining to each other about all the chores we had to do.

Dennis said, "I'd like to run away, then I wouldn't have to do anything I didn't want to do." The more we thought about running away, the better it sounded! We started making plans. "I have six dollars and fifty-four cents," I volunteered. Dennis said, "I've got almost eleven dollars." "We could always pick up discarded pop cans and other things to recycle to get more money," I exclaimed. "Boy, I like the sound of this more and more all the time!" "Where will we live if we run away?" I wondered out loud. "What about our old club house?" said Dennis. "Great!" we shouted.

We both went home and packed our things. I left a note for my parents, saying that I didn't live there anymore. I wrote that I was moving in with Dennis at our old club house in the vacant lot behind Elmer's Market. I packed up two pairs of levis, four pairs of socks, three t-shirts, my summer jacket, a pillow and a blanket. I threw in a few of my favorite books and a flashlight. I tied my things on my bicycle and left!

When I got to the club house, I put my things away and waited for Dennis. He came shortly after and put his things away, too. "Now what will we do?" we said. "We can do anything we want. No more big people telling us what we had to do!"

"Let's go to the store and get something to eat," I said. "I'm hungry." So we did. We bought different kinds of candy bars, 6 cans of root beer and the same amount of orange soda. We bought chocolate donuts and Twinkies. We decided that we might as well buy something nutritious, so we bought a couple of cartons of milk. We got up to the check-out stand and all our stuff came to almost twenty dollars. We decided to take back the cartons of milk because they might go sour before we'd get a chance to drink them.

We went back to the club house. We sat around eating candy and donuts. I had a root beer and Dennis had an orange soda. We told jokes, wrestled each other and played a little basketball with the garbage can and candy wrappers. We both read for a while. I let Dennis use some of my books because he forgot to bring his.

I had another donut and Dennis had some more candy. We didn't drink any more pop because it was already kind of warm and we didn't have a refrigerator to put them in to get them cold. Our stomachs started feeling a little woozie, so we decided we needed something more nutritious.

We didn't have enough money so we took the plastic bag our groceries came in and went out gathering up cans to earn more money to buy some milk. We gathered a lot, we thought, but when we took them to the store, we didn't earn enough, so we went back to our club house home. "We're going to have to find some kind of job other than just collection cans if we're going to have anything to eat," we both agreed.

It was starting to get dark. I was the only one with a flashlight. "What if the batteries went out on us?" I asked and then said, "We had better use it sparingly." That's about the time we both started wondering what was going on with our family at our "used to be home".

Without saying another word, we gathered up our stuff. We took off out the door, tied our stuff back on our bicycles and made for a return trip to, you guessed it, home!

When I got home, the lights were all on. I went to go right in but then I remembered the note that I left saying I no longer lived there. I rang the doorbell. Dad came to the door. "Well, well, well," he said, "and who do we have here?" I asked him if he needed another boy to help with chores and such, since his son had run off. He said in a very serious voice, "I think so but let me check with my wife first."

Mom came and dad told her what I wanted. Mom said in her serious voice, too, "Well, (pause) I don't know." Then, they both laughed and gave me the biggest hug.

It was great being home again, chores and everything else. I really missed the "everything else"!

Follow-Up Activities for "Runaways"

Pretend you are one of the two boys in the story. Fill out this "Interest Inventory" as you think he would if he were doing it.

1. If I had all the money I could ever want I would

2. When I grow up I will

3. In school the thing I like to do best is

4. My most favorite person in the whole world is

5. My favorite place to be is

6. My favorite television show is

7. I like to play

8. When I am all alone I like to

9. The best book I've ever read is

10. Things that make me laugh are

11. In summer time I like to

12. If I could have any pet I wanted, it would be a

13. The things that I dislike most are

14. The sport that I like to watch best is

15. The sport that I am best in is

16. I would like to have a collection of

17. Other interesting things about me

WRITING PROMPT: Make a list of chores that you like to do by yourself and a list that you like to do with someone else. Now make a list of chores you do not like to do by yourself or with someone else.

Smudge the Cat

Marissa was playing outside one day when she heard a strange sound coming from underneath a bush. She listened closer. It was a soft meowing. It stopped, then she heard it again.

Marissa carefully parted the bushes and looked inside. She saw a fuzzy, gray bundle of fur cowering under some leaves. "Come here, kitty," she called quietly, so as not to scare the cat. It didn't move. She called it again, this time moving a bit closer. The cat moved back nervously, but eventually allowed Marissa to stroke it's soft fur. "Come on kitty, I won't hurt you," she whispered, and with that, she put her hand around the cat's body and gently pulled him out. Surprisingly, he did not struggle.

Marissa looked at him closely. He seemed weak and tired. His whiskers were covered with dirt and he had a small scratch on his face. She decided to take him home and clean him up.

She walked around the block to her home. "Mom," Marissa called out. "Look what I found!" Marissa's mother sighed. Marissa was always bringing home hurt or lost animals. It was almost as if the animals knew how to find her. She admired Marissa's compassion and they had had such luck in finding the animal's owners in the past. Maybe, they would find this cat's owner, too.

Marissa and her mother cleaned out the cat's cut and brushed his fur. They gave him some water, food and a soft place to sleep. They then called the newspaper and placed an advertisement about the lost animal. Marissa was sad because she really liked this cat. He was sweet and friendly. He seemed to like her, too. She secretly hoped that no one would claim him.

Two days later, they got a phone call. "Hello, I'm calling about the lost cat," the woman said. "Can you describe him?" Marissa's mother asked. The woman described her cat and asked if she could come over to see him. Marissa's mother said, "That would be fine."

An hour later, the woman rang Marissa's doorbell. "Hello," the woman said. "I'm here to see Smudge." "Smudge?" Marissa said. "Yes, that's what I call him," the woman answered. "When we found him three years ago, he had smudges of black soot all over his body. So we call him Smudge. Can I see him?"

Marissa reluctantly brought the woman to where Smudge was sleeping. "Yes, that's him," the woman said. Then she looked at Marissa, who had tears in her eyes. "What's the matter?" the woman asked. "Well, it's just that I really like your cat and will miss him when he's gone," Marissa replied.

The woman thought a moment. She said, "I'll make you a deal. I'm not home very much, so it's hard for me to give Smudge the attention he needs. I only live a few blocks away. Will you be able to come over everyday to play with him?" That made Marissa very happy. She agreed and from then on, Marissa and Smudge were the best of friends!

Jorgie's Jive

Have you kept a list of your favorite stories?
It would be fun to share your list with your friends.

Follow-Up Activities for "Smudge the Cat"

1. **Using complete sentences, write five facts about Smudge.**
    A.
    B.
    C.
    D.
    E.

2. **Write five facts about Marissa using complete sentences.**
    A.
    B.
    C.
    D.
    E.

3. **Match the parts of speech by drawing a line from the word to it's definition.**

    noun   * is an action word, tells what something is, was or will be

    pronoun   * describes a noun or a pronoun

    verb   * names a person, place or thing

    adjective   * describes a verb. May answer how, when, or where

    adverb   * takes the place of a noun

4. **Put a circle around the word in each sentence that the "Parts of Speech" word calls for.**

    A. (noun) Marissa careful parted the bushes.
    B. (verb) She brought home lots of lost animals.
    C. (pronoun) "Come on kitty," she whispered.
    D. (adjective) The gray kitten was scared.
    E. (adverb) Smudge moved nervously towards Marissa.
    F. (pronoun) Marissa and her mother took good care of him.
    G. (verb) The bundle of fir was under some leaves.
    H. (adjective) The tall woman laughed out loud.
    I. (noun) The angry man kicked the dirt.
    J. (adverb) Marissa often cries when she's sad.

WRITING PROMPT: Pretend that you have found a lost animal. Write an advertisement for your local newspaper about the animal. Use a lot of descriptive words!

The Snow Maiden *A Russian Fairy Tale*

Many years ago there lived an old woman and an old man. As they grew older and older, they also grew sadder and sadder, for they had no children.

One winter morning, the old man looked out the window and saw snow falling. It kept falling and falling. Soon he saw some boys and girls playing outside, sliding on their sleds and throwing snowballs. After a while, they all began making a snowman.

As the old man was watching them, he turned to the old woman and said, "let us go outside and make a snowman too." "Very well," said the old woman, "but instead, let us make a little daughter out of snow, a snow maiden." So they did.

They went out into the garden and began to make a little girl out of snow. They made the legs, the arms and the head. They used bits of sparkling ice for the eyes, and they even made the eyebrows.

When the old man and old woman had finished, they could hardly believe that they had made such a beautiful snow maiden.

Suddenly, the snow maiden began to smile; she moved her eyebrows, she raised her arms and then she began to walk quietly along the snow toward the hut.

The old man and old woman were overjoyed and they ran after her into the hut. They did not know where to begin to prepare for their guest.

This little snow maiden stayed and lived with the old man and the old woman. Each day she became more lovely and more dear.

The days passed, until winter came to an end and spring arrived. The sun began to warm the earth. The water in the brooks began to flow from under the snow. Water began to drip from the roofs. All the children were joyous at the coming of spring. The snow maiden was unhappy and sat in her hut and would not look out the window.

Summer arrived, the sun was hot and flowers were blooming. The snow maiden was afraid to step outside the door. She would not go out, but the old woman persuaded her to. "Go on, little daughter. Why do you shut yourself in all alone?"

The snow maiden obeyed and went off with some girls who were playing outside. They were having a great time. Even though they were not suppose to, they built a bonfire. One of them got the dangerous idea of jumping over the flames. She jumped and then another jumped and then a third.

"Why don't you jump?" her friends said to her. "Or are you afraid?" They began to laugh at her.

She gathered courage and jumped. The girls watched, but where was the snow maiden? She had disappeared! There was only a white mist above the bonfire. The mist formed into a thin cloud and rose higher and higher until it joined the clouds in the sky.

The old man and the old woman wept bitterly when their dear little snow maiden did not return. They looked for her everywhere and waited for her every night. They were sad and lonely, talking and thinking only about their little daughter they had loved so much.

After a while, the days became shorter and the nights longer. The air was crisp and cool once again. Winter was coming.

One night, when the first snow was falling, they heard a happy laugh outside their hut and a dear familiar voice singing,

"Winter is here. I am back with the snow.
But please do not fear, in summer when I go."

They ran to the door, and there was their little daughter, their snow maiden. How happy they all were to be together again! She stayed with them all winter long and played with the other children of the village.

When summer came she disappeared and the cycle continued in the winter when she returned. The old man and the old woman knew not to be so sad because she would return when the snow began to fall, bringing them joy and happiness!

Follow-Up Activities for "The Snow Maiden"

Answer these in complete sentences:

1. Why did the old man and old woman want to make a snow maiden?

2. Why was the snow maiden sad when spring came?

3. Sometimes friends do things together that are unsafe or not wise and try to persuade other to follow them. Can you think of a time when this has happened to you? Explain.

4. What happened to the snow maiden when she jumped over the fire?

5. Why could the snow maiden come back?

6. Read the sentences. Circle each verb and then write the past tense form of it above the word.

   1. The small sailboats came to the dock.
   2. James and David tug hard at the kite.
   3. The scouts play in the dark room.
   4. The insects fly to the garden plants.
   5. Mark reads his library book every night.
   6. Samantha tries to smile because she's brave.
   7. She gives Mrs. Olsen a basket of flowers.
   8. Natalie goes up to the pitcher's mound.

WRITING PROMPT: Write a fairy tale about a dinosaur or other extinct animal that lives in your backyard or neighborhood.

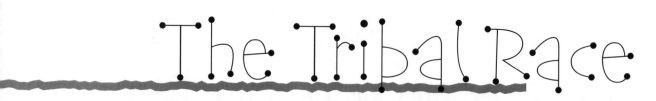

This summer was the summer with grandpa and the old ways. Grandpa lived in the Northern mountains of Mexico. My father had grown up there and so had his father's father, back til he could no longer remember the telling of tribal life.

My father had lived there as a small boy. As he grew older, he was sent away to school to study and learn other ways. There he met and married my mother and stayed there. My sister and I returned to the mountain home of my father and grandfather on rare occasions.

This summer, I was old enough to spend the whole summer with grandfather! My grandfather and I wrote letters anticipating our time together. My father and grandfather had spoken of traditions and of the old ways to me many times. This was my chance to experience some of it first-hand.

Time came, I said good-bye to my family and my city dwelling for a time.

That evening, grandfather and I sat by an open fire. Grandfather asked about my trip, about my life at school and my family. All the while he talked, he carved. As he carved, the shape opened up.

Grandfather usually carved beautiful animals but this was curiously round like a ball, a wooden ball. I questioned grandfather. It was then that he told me of the tribal race of the "fast runners."

As a young man, my grandfather apparently had run many

such races, becoming one of the best know of the tribe. The object of the race was to run the course, kicking the ball with one foot as you went. If you kicked the ball too far or too fast and lost it, you had to find it or get another, before you could proceed on.

In my grandfather's time and his father's time as far back as could be remembered, it was not unusual to run for two days and two nights along mountainous terrain. I was totally amazed that such a feat could ever have been. I could never imagine myself doing such a thing.

I asked my grandfather if the race was still being performed in the tribe. My grandfather's eyes twinkled as his reply was, "Yes, grandson and I am carving a foot racing ball just for you!" "Oh, no grandfather, you can't be serious. I could never run such a race!"

"We have all summer to decide," he said, "besides the race is only five miles long now days." This made me feel a little better because I was one of the fastest runners at home, on the track team.

My grandfather taught me many things that summer. He taught me of the old ways. He told me stories of long ago, each night as we sat by the open fire.

The most memorable part of the day and the most difficult for me, was to practice running with the ball in front of me. I was very awkward and clumsy at first. It took me days and days to get the hang of it.

The other boys laughed at my clumsiness. They taunted me and called me "fumble paw." "Look at ol' 'fumble paw,' can't run as good as his grandpa." I felt humiliated and close to tears many time.

I kept trying with my grandfather's encouragement. I was determined to give it my best. I practiced every chance I got. I even ran at night, with the stars and moon as my guide. Eventually, I felt like I had finally got the hang of it.

The day of the race came! I nervously stood on the starting line. The signal was given and the race was on! Many of the villagers ran behind us to see how well we were doing and to cheer us on!

I must show my grandfather that I can do this. I said to myself. Run , run, faster, faster. Be careful, don't loose the ball. I was close to the finish line, a short space ahead of all the rest except one, when I stumbled and fell flat on my face.

"I lost," I cried,, "I wanted to make you proud. I wanted to be the best, like you, grandpa."

My grandfather helped me up saying, "I lost many times before I won. You are not a loser. You did your best. I am so proud of you. Your first race like this and you were so close! You are a winner, learning!"

I promised myself right there and then that when I went home, the "kicking ball" would go with me, that when I return to be with grandfather, I would run with the wind and make him proud!

Follow-Up Activities for "The Tribal Race"

1. Find and write the words in the story that mean the same as:

    A. unusual _____   B. looking forward_____

    C. customs _____   D. home _____

    E. interested to know ____   F. clan_____

    G. obviously _____   H. surface features _____

    I. surprised _____   J. function _____

    K. sparkle _____   L. response_____

    M. notable _____   N. hard_____

    O. lacking dexterity _____   P. mortified _____

    Q. made fun of _____   R. resolved _____

    S. inspire _____   T. apprehensive _____

    U. vowed_____   Z. self-respect_____

2. Punctuate these sentences correctly:

    A. I am going to my friends house

    B. Wow thats really really great

    C. What kind of sandwich do you have in your lunch

    D. My mother told me that youre moving

    E. Why are you moving so far away

    F. Ill come and visit you next summer

3. Write a short paragraph using complete sentences about how the boy felt when he fell and then how he felt after his grandfather discussed it with him.

Writing Prompt: Write a story about a Native American child going back in a time capsule to the early days. Write about how he/she felt and what he/she did. How he/she tried to explain the future and how he/she lives.

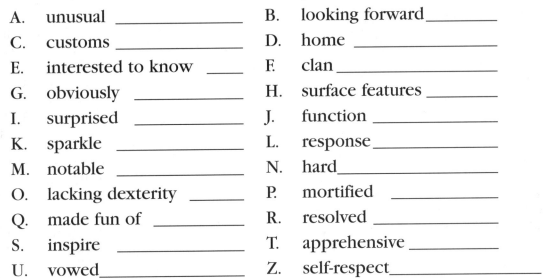

If

If life was like your imagination,
How strange your house would Be!

The roof would be low,
The floor would be high
The walls would stretch tall,
Right up to the sky!

If life was like your imagination,
How odd your reflection would be!

Your nose would stretch far away from your face,
Your legs would be vines, growing at a great pace!
Your clothes, so many colors,
not one of them matched,

Your torso sprouting wings,
like birds recently hatched!

If life was like your imagination,
How unusual the world would be!
Townspeople would fly and birds would stay put

Sunrise would come second,
sundown would be first

Candy would spring both from ground
and from trees
And children would rule earth's many countries

If like was like your imagination,
How wonderful it would be.
So shut your eyes,
And think of a place
Where your imagination can run free!

After reading the poem do the following:

1. Write a description of what life would be like if life was like your imagination.
    Illustrate it.

SUMMER NOTES:

Make a list of your five favorites stories in this book, then write a sentence which tells why you liked them.

Do any of the stories remind you of places, things or animals you like? For example if you'd like cats then maybe "Smudge the Cat," was your favorite story!

Answer Sheets

Answers Will Vary in all Writing Prompts Exercises

1. **The Stray Hero:**
Definitions: stray - wondered off, exhausting - tired out, mangy - scruffy, pathetic - pitiful, refuge - shelter, disturbed - interrupted.
Correct verb: had, ran, got, was, took, seen, give, came
Nouns: ham, sandwich, mother, elephant, celery, mustard, seasons, wonder, animals, vet, water, money, face, tongue, hero, friend
Next three answers may vary: Dad thought someone would claim the kitten. He did not want to be bothered besides he was too tired. To get rid of the gas fumes and to let in some fresh air.

2. **Going to Work With Dad:** Answers may vary somewhat.
Maybe David didn't see the need for school. David wanted to be an architect. One ticket to get there and one to come home on. Difference: apartments, shopping malls, taxies, peanut vendors. Dad's office building that overlooked the city. In the morning. The train rocked David to sleep because he was tired. Doing well in school is important in achieving.
Endings: Answers will vary. shopper, entered, playing, bought, exclaimed, walker, chugging, smiled popped, dancing, asked, watched, tourist, exits, gentlest, opener, wants, leaving, harden, decided, whistled, sharing, climber, replying.
Mainly about: Going to work with Dad.

3. **"Wannabe:"**
Fill in the blanks: alternative, discouraged, selection, commented, hobbled, perspective, suggestions, comfortable, neighborhood, exceptional.
Scrambled words: wise, clever, mysterious, happy, sad, mean, foolish, kind, strange, cruel, funny, friendly, sneaky, generous.
Homographs: Answers will vary.
Example: apples cost 10cents a pound. I took my hammer to pound the nail in.

4. **Time and Place**
Alphabetical order: animals, culture, customs, firedrill, flowers, football, friends, grandparents, picnics, recess, reportcards, science, soccer, swimming.
Opposites: Answers may vary. sunny - cloudy, discussing - argue, growing - shrinking, vacation - work, prepare - unprepared, harvest - plant, grandparents - grandchildren, changes - same, winter - summer, receive - give.

5. **Moving to the Big Apple:** Answers to the first three situations will vary.
Words that don't belong: sleeping, upsetting, leave, reject, scramble, backward, sent.
Correct endings: angrier, happily, stories, movers, stairs, best, staying/summer, adventures, friendship, offered.

6. **Grandpa Remembers**
Sequence: 5, 1, 3, 6, 2, 4, 7,
Prefixes: Answers will vary. presoak, triangle, unlock, tricycle, unusual, redo, proclaim,

postcard, program, discourage, posthole, recount, postpone, recreate, unzip, bypass, preside, intrude, present, remake, record, disagree, unwanted, byway.

I or Me: I, me, I, , I, me, me

Contrations: Answers may vary. He's, he'll, You're, I'm, she's, You've, We'll, let's

7. **Trapped Beneath**

   Words: trap, consent, wrecked, clung, aparently, delivered, allusive, noticed, grin, concern.

   Advice: Stay together and keep track of how much oxygen you have left.

   Why: Answers may vary. Because they ate lobsters or because they earned money by selling lobsters.

   Past verbs: enjoyed, swept, stretched, sent, threw, pushed, dusted , pulled, touched, knew, sat, left, caught, hugged, poured, spoke, swam, kept, imagined, sled, spoke, joined, demanded, fought, built, touched, poured, thought, wrote, carried.

   Finish the Sentences: Answers will vary.

8. **The New kid**

   Answers will vary for # 1, 2, 3, 4

   Compound words: Answers will vary. graveyard, lightbulb, ditchbank, fingernail, grasshopper, reportcard, somewhere, careless, windmill, shoelace, waterfall, housecoat, mailbox, downstairs, grapevine, notebook, bathtub, doorknob, blackboard, clothescloset, football, rainbow, nightmare, background, birdbath, peanut, postcard, sandwich, superman, anyhow, bookstore, starfish.

9. **Heroes**: **Add "ing:"** stopping, making, treating, coming.

   Homonym: sun

   Rhyming: me-be, fly-try. **Lemonade Stand answers will vary.**

10. **Skipping rocks**

    Other sports: Answers will vary. racing, jumping, swimming, birdwatching, etc.

    Word group sequence: 2 - 1 - 3, 2 - 3 - 1, 1 -2 - 3, 3 - 2 - 1, 2 - 1 - 3 , 1 - 2 - 3, 2 - 1 - 3, 3 - 2 - 1, 3 - 1 - 2, 1 - 3 - 2

    Possessive Pronouns: Answers will vary.

11. **The County Fair:** Answers to numbers 1 and 2 will vary.

    Fair Barkers: people who work at the fair, that call out to you to ride the rides or to play the games.

    Synonyms - Answers may vary. plentiful

    Antonyms - answers may vary. scarce

12. **Visiting Dr. White**

    Word Referents: run, black dog, little sister, Sam and Sara, Frank, fence, Myra and Skip, Dr. White,   Robert and Zelma, sun.

    Syllables: 2, 3, 2, 2, 3, 1, 1, 2, 2, 3, 1, 4, 2, 2, 5, 1, 1, 1, 2, 5, 3, 2, 3, 2, 2, 2, 2,

    Complete the words: place, present, photo, prase, problem, phantom, planets, plot, prize, gopher, reply, prove, improve, trophy, surprise, supply, nephew, geography, airplane, apron, approach, telegraph, autograph, complain, apply, impression express, perplex, triumph

Answer Sheets

13. What's That Noise:
   1. Fools gold or silver. It was in veins and glistened. 2. A bear, or some type of animal 3. Answer will vary. 4. Answer will vary.
   Correct Vowel: admit, ugly, beggar, other, stop, scrap, signal, admit, fond, uncle, whip, step, peanut, season, sketch, upset, graduate, bedbug, dugout, bunch, itch, flat, blot, wet.
   Correct Vowels: toad, beat, speak, beach, deal, team, grown, tried, toast, nail, goat, pea, dream, daisy, approach, foam, snail, please, croak, load, aid, cheap, spied, plead, dead.

14. Breakfast
   Sequence: (answers going across) 6, 4, 1, 8, 10, 2, 9, 3, 7, 5. Fruit, cereal, toast, bagels, etc. Cake, pie, candy

15. Sweet Porridge, A fairy Tale Answers to # 1, 2, 3, 4 will vary
   Silent letters: would   write   could   know   back   through   right   answer   should   high   light   thought   might   aften   night   walk   enough   watch   talk   knew

16. Neighborhood Reporters
   Sequence of events: 2, 1, 5, 3, 7, 4, 6
   Correct Meanings: A - 4, 7, 1, 8,   10, 2, 3, 5, 9, 6   B - 8, 10, 1, 3, 7, 9, 4, 6, 2, 5
   C - 3, 6, 1, 2, 4, 8, 10, 7, 5, 9   D - 6, 1, 8, 3, 4, 9, 10, 2, 5, 7

17. Neighborhood Watch
   Important facts: Answers may vary somewhat. Men were taking things that did not belong to them.   Knew the Walker's were out of town.   Told them the name and address.   Described the men and what they were wearing.   Described the van and part of the license numbers.   Stayed out of sight and safe.   Watched where the men went when they drove off.
   Dangerous situation: Answers will vary. The thieves could have seen them. They needed to stay undectected.
   Belong together: Answers will vary. dress, football, lemonade, biscuits, radishes, grapes, lake, plate, rake   ears.

18. Riddle Me This
   Rhyming words: cat - bat - rat - that, be - me - flea - bee - we,   shark - lark - dark,   train - plane - rain,   chugger - bugger,   dad - Brad,   Paul - haul - call, bend - end.
   Riddles: newspaper, potato, cow - goat - deer - moose, flowerbed
   Answers to numbers 3 and 4 will vary

19. Surprise on a Snowy Saturday
   Sentences that tell about the story: 2, 4, 5, 6, 8, 10 **Answers may vary for #1 and 2.**
   1. Chuck laughed and kept trying. His brother said that he was doing great; 2. He saw some kids his age that flew right past him; 3. Chuck and his brother snowboarding; 4. Chuck's Big Day; 5. He didn't give up when he fell; 6. All the things listed are important.

20. Friday
   Answers will vary for # 1,2,3

1. She could swim much faster than she used to. She had won ten ribbons already. She felt strong and the coach had complimented her.   2. Laura was the last person out of the pool and the last one to line up. "Do it again," said Coach. "I can't," said Laura.   3. Because he knew Laura could do it.

Correct Homonyms: **A** - 7, 4, 5, 11, 1, 2, 8, 3, 6, 9, 10.   **B** - 3, 6, 4, 1, 9, 10, 8, 7, 5, 2, 11   **C** - 3, 1, 2, 5, 8, 11, 4, 10, 9, 7, 6   **D** - 2, 9, 7, 11, 1, 3, 4, 10, 8, 6, 5

21. Oh Where Are We Going?
Rhyming pairs: going - knowing, yard - hard, stream - dream, shade - unafraid, wrong - song, away - play, sea - free, sky - why, blue - you, calls - falls,   time - climb, sets - yet, gone - long. **Homonym:** blue - blew, high - hi, you - ewe, right - write.
Root word: afraid, seek, tend, turn, know, advent or vent, pirate, be. **Fiction:** elves, fairies

22. If I were 1. Pick themselves up when they stumble, try their best, take action, take time for kindness and friendships. 2. Giving, good example, courageous. 3. Act naturally and people will love you for you. 4. asking, advantage, ordinary, back, give, working, willing, unknowingly.

23. Runaways: Answers will vary

24. Smudge the Cat
Facts about Smudge: Answers will vary some. Smudge was covered with dirt. Smudge had a scratch on his face. He is a gray cat. He belongs to a lady. Smudge was lost three years ago. Facts about Marissa's Answers may vary. She loves animals. She brings home hurt or lost animals. She likes Smudge. She helps her Mom take care of the cat's injuries. She cries when she is sad.
Parts of Speech: Noun - names a person place or thing. Pronoun - takes the place of a noun. Verb - is an action word, tells what something is, was, or will be. Adjective - describes a noun or a pronoun. Adverb - describes a verb. May answer how, when or where.
Parts of Speech: Marissa, brought, she, gray, nervously, her, under, tall, man, often.

25. The Snow Maiden, A Russian Fairy Tale: Answers will vary.
1. They wanted a child of their own. 2. She was afraid to go outside because it was getting warm 3. Answers will vary. 4. The snow maiden disappeared. 5. She came back because it was cold again and because this is a fairy tale.
Verbs: present to past tense. came - come tug - tugged play - played fly - flew reads - read tries - tried gives - gave goes - went

26. The Tribal Race
Similiar Words: rare, anticipating, traditions, dwelling,   curiously,   tribe or tribal, apparently, mountainous, terrain, amazed, performed, twinkled, reply, memorable, difficult, clumsy, humiliated, taunted, determined, encouraged, nervously, promised, proud.
Punctuation: May vary somewhat. 1. friend's . 2. Wow, that's really, !   3. ? 4. you're . 5. ? 6. I'll ! **Paragraph** - Answers will vary.

27. If: Answers will vary.

SUMMER JOURNAL:

Keep a daily journal describing your summer days on these pages.
You can also write a story about your favorite day. Have fun!

Thanks for sharing your summer with me! I hope you had a great one! Do your best in school, learning is important.

See you next year, JORGiE

Certificate of Completion

Awarded to

Name

"My brain is bigger now that I have completed Summer Bridge Reading Activities!"

George Starks

George Starks, Creative Director

Parent's Signature